# HOW TO AVOID
# HUGE SHIPS

# HOW TO AVOID
# HUGE SHIPS
## AND OTHER
## IMPLAUSIBLY TITLED BOOKS

## INTRODUCTION BY
## Joel Rickett

First published in Great Britain 2008
by Aurum Press Ltd
7 Greenland Street
London NW1 0ND
www.aurumpress.co.uk

A catalogue record for this book is available
from the British Library.

ISBN 978 1 84513 321 4

10 9 8 7 6 5 4 3 2
2012  2011  2010  2009  2008

Design by Isobel Gillan
Printed in Slovenia

# INTRODUCTION

'Glory be to God for dappled things …
All things counter, original, spare, strange.'
*Gerard Manley Hopkins, 'Pied Beauty' (1918)*

WHAT MAKES A BOOK TITLE TRULY ODD? I don't mean merely quaint, funny or outlandish; I mean utterly, remarkably, jaw-droppingly bizarre. Scientists have toiled for years researching this question; perhaps the answer will always remain elusive. Yet we instantly recognize oddness when we see it. For example, take a book such as *Bombproof Your Horse*. If the authors had opted for an alternative equestrian title (*Train Your Horse*, say) their work would never have raised eyebrows.

After wading through thousands of odd book titles for this seminal collection, I believe that a degree of ignorance is essential. The writers and publishers must be oblivious to the sheer queerness of their choice, usually because they are so close to the subject that they cannot see its absurdity. Take the photographer who lovingly documented the strange skin decorations and ornaments he found in a far-flung land. He believed there was only one choice when titling the resulting book: *Tattooed Mountain Women and Spoon Boxes of Daghestan*. Or recall the British Crop Protection Council researcher who believed his study needed a visionary title, opting for *Weeds in a Changing World*. Often writers miss the potential double meaning of their masterpiece. When the European Commission's top physicists were compiling recent developments in steel research, they had no qualms about calling the resulting book *The Physical Properties of Slags*.

For thirty years the oddest of these odd titles have been found and celebrated by the *Bookseller* magazine's Diagram Prize for Oddest Book Title of the Year. Forget the Booker, the Nobel or the Pulitzer: real book lovers and the literati agree that the Diagram transcends them all. Every year entries flood in from around the world, starting a spell of frenzied voting and blanket media coverage.

This hunt for 'unlikely' book titles was originally suggested by publisher Bruce Robertson as a diversion for bored visitors to the Frankfurt Book Fair. For the uninitiated, Frankfurt is a kind of global clearing house for books, a soulless collection of giant sheds with hundreds of thousands of titles on display. Robertson hoped his wheeze would provide publishers with a moment's diversion while plodding the aisles, a way to avoid those chain-smoking continental editors and cigar-chomping Americans. His idea was simple but effective. Many of the earliest discoveries were by no means vintage – the best were *100 Years of British Rail Catering*, *Cooking with God*, and *50 New Poodle Grooming Styles*. But there was a single standout title: *Proceedings of the Second International Workshop on Nude Mice*, published by the University of Tokyo Press. The Diagram Prize was born.

The Frankfurt Book Fair has been running since the twelfth century. It is intriguing to imagine what would have been discovered by, say, Martin Luther, if he had been scouring the stands for odd titles. Certainly we know that spotters in the nineteenth century would have been spoilt for choice; the Victorians blended objective enquiry with a gruesome oddness. Three classics that immediately come to mind are *Dentologia: A Poem on the Diseases of the Teeth*, *Premature Burial and How It May Be Prevented*, and *The Romance of Leprosy*.

From the early days the procedures of the Diagram Prize appear to have been deliberately vague. Run by the *Bookseller* magazine's diarist Horace Bent, a legendary book-trade figure, the winners seem to have been settled by an elite, anonymous group, probably over port at a London club. Any type of book was admissible, with the only restriction being that publishers were not allowed to submit their own books, to screen out intentional efforts at oddness. In 1993 submissions were opened beyond the confines of Frankfurt: immediately readers of the *Bookseller* (bookshop staff, academics, editors, librarians and literary agents) started scanning through the endless lists of new titles. As publishing output spiralled, there were rich pickings. And when the major publishing corporations tried to squeeze any remaining oddness out of the industry, digital printing technology sprung up, enabling quirkier small publishers to produce books for niche interests (no matter how specific). The Diagram judges resisted the temptation to allow books from vanity presses – it would be too easy for people to invent odd titles just to win the prize. All shortlisted books must be properly published, in a bid to reach a defined – if elusive – audience.

Merrily scanning the lists of Diagram Prize winners and runners-up, it is clear that the gloriously sincere endeavours of medical research have provided one of the richest seams over the thirty years. Just imagine leafing through some of these suggestively titled works: *A Pictorial Book of Tongue*

*Coatings*, *A Colour Atlas of Posterior Chamber Implants*, or *Inflammatory Bowel Diseases: A Personal View*. Being so obsessed with their narrow field of research, medical authors often seem to miss ambiguity. So *Practical Infectious Diseases* was presumably not a how-to guide to infecting your enemies, while the 2003 favourite *Hot Topics in Urology* sounds painfully relevant.

Nature's glories have often been celebrated in book form. I imagine that there was an avid, if specialist, readership for *Six-Legged Sex: The Erotic Lives of Bugs*, as well as *Neurosis Induced Cannibalism in Antarctic Pigs* (brilliantly edited by Pigman Press). Farmers everywhere presumably flocked to bookshops to snap up a copy of *The Potatoes of Bolivia: Their Breeding, Value and Evolutionary Relationships*. That's if the Celtic ones weren't already busy reading (and perhaps road-testing) the very personal manual titled *Sex Instructions for Irish Farmers*.

Every respectable household still has its fair share of 'how-to' and hobby books; perhaps your own shelves include *Drying Flowers With a Microwave*, or *Waterproofing Your Child*. You are less likely to have a copy of the rare 1989 Diagram winner, *How to Shit in the Woods*, which was aimed at people who needed an entire book to learn this 'lost art'. And what gentleman could live without the *Braces Owners Manual: A Guide to the Wearing and Care of Braces*, or the essential companion to facial hygiene that is *Nasal Maintenance*? To our enlightened ears, some of the books published in an earlier age can sound morally dubious. But we must be careful not to judge the men who, in the early 1980s, followed the advice set out in *Wife Battering: A Systems Theory Approach*. Perhaps their spouses took revenge by learning from the classic *Interpersonal Violence: The Practical Series*.

As with any high-profile literary award, controversies have rocked the Diagram over the years. There were several dark stretches where no prize was awarded at all (who could imagine the Booker Prize admitting that no novel was worthy of the accolade?). When public voting was introduced in 2000 – via the newfangled interweb – the prize's custodian Horace Bent threatened to resign. How could his impeccable judgement be disregarded in favour of the teeming multitudes? However, despite his outburst reaching the diary columns of the national newspapers, Mr Bent failed to carry out his promise, and eventually contented himself with drawing up the short list and giving most publicity to his favoured titles. I refuse to believe the rumours of bribery and rigged polling.

The Diagram is unique, and perhaps uniquely blessed, in that spotters and judges alike do not actually have to read the books in question. Indeed they are actively discouraged from doing so, in case a close knowledge of the subject makes them realize the book is less odd than it first appears. The imagination should be allowed to run wild, particularly with those books which seem preoccupied with blindingly obvious topics. Why, we wonder, did the author need so many pages to explain the art of *Big and Very Big Hole Drilling*? And why did the writer believe people required an entire book on his *Method For Calculating the Size of Stone Needed for Closing End-Tipped Rubble Banks in Rivers*? Did the level of local interest really merit an entire tome about the question *Did Lewis Carroll Visit Llandudno?* Surely a simple yes or no would have sufficed.

Sometimes this habit of using an entire book to tackle a single issue seems positively reckless. When the captain of your little pleasure cruiser spots a ferry hull looming over the horizon, do you really want him to reach for a copy of *How to Avoid Huge Ships*? Or would you rather that he kept his attentions on the wheel?

It is inevitable that some of the oddest winning titles appeal to our basest emotions, but new depths have been plumbed in the last decade. The first suggestive title was *Archaeology in the American Bottom* in 1993 (was that book about real excavations in the posteriors of American citizens, or is bottom archaeology an American skill to be explained and exported?). In 1997 came the highly creative *The Joy of Sex: Pocket Edition*. But in 2000 the vulgarities of public voting ushered in the most debased winner yet: an engineering manual called *High Performance Stiffened Structures*. It is also worth noting a repeated fascination with lesbianism, which some readers clearly still find adds an extra level of oddity. So we have 1990's *Lesbian Sadomasochism Safety Manual*, as well as the 2003 champion, *The Big Book of Lesbian Horse Stories*.

Winning the Diagram brings no immediate monetary reward for the author; instead it is the spotter of the title who receives a bottle of the 'fairly passable' (usually claret). But most winning authors have been delighted at the accolade and the ensuing media attention. From the *Sun* to the *Ohio Journal*, from Russian state media to the BBC World Service, the prize is obsessively reported (and journalists have tried flattery and subterfuge in failed bids to discover the name of the winner before the official announcement). Such publicity can transform the profile of a title, lifting it from academic obscurity to the front of bookshops. The 2006 winner, *The Stray Shopping Carts of Eastern North America: A Guide to Field Identification*, was displayed in stores across the world, its grateful author inundated with offers of interviews. Such coverage has drawn the attention of major corporations, keen to sponsor the award and boost their public image. But unlike the Booker and the Orange Prize, the Diagram has refused all such blandishments: it must retain a higher purity of purpose, unsullied by commercial concerns.

While publishers are not allowed to enter their own titles, the match of title and publishing house is often intriguing. Why did the University of Chicago Press take such interest in releasing a work of trans-European history called *Versailles: The View from Sweden*? Others are more apt: Transaction Press published the essential guidebook *The Madam as Entrepreneur: Career Management in House Prostitution*, while the British Cement Association surely had a vested interest in releasing *Highlights in the History of Concrete* and their other classic, *Lakeside Car Parks*. And when he had completed a reference volume about *Greek Rural Postmen and Their Cancellation Numbers*, who else could the author send his manuscript to but the Hellenic Philatelic Society?

The Diagram Prize's reach is not all-encompassing; some gems take years to come to light. For instance, in 1988 the prize overlooked a classic: *The Gut Contents of Six Leathery Turtles*. But I have subsequently discovered that the world of turtle research is a fertile source of odd titles. There's the useful *Plastic Bags in the Intestinal Tracts of Leatherback Marine Turtles*, or the improbable-sounding *Transatlantic*

*Travel by Juvenile Loggerhead Turtle*. There's also a turtle-related tract called *Rips, Fads, and Little Loggerheads*.

Sometimes odd titles can uncover whole new worlds. Take *Proceedings of the 18th International Seaweed Symposium*. Who would have known that since 1973, scientists have been meeting regularly to discuss pressing developments in seaweed (the next Seaweed Symposium is scheduled for Mexico 2010). I wonder if the same commitment has been shown in other fields. Did *Proceedings of the Sixth International Fatigue Congress* have any sequels, or did the participants all grow tired of the ritual?

It's all too easy to sneer at some of these books. But oddness is in the eye of the beholder. Thanks to amazon.com we discover that some readers loved *The Stray Shopping Carts of Eastern North America*: a certain S. Fragomen hails it as a 'hilariously depressing work', while A.J. Fries observes that 'the author's language coupled with his beautiful photography give the lowly carts individual personalities'. And while *People Who Don't Know They're Dead* picked up some terrible reviews, the book helped Mr Jeffrey Duncan: 'It sheds light on an area of the paranormal not often discussed, the idea of hitchhiker spirits … I felt as if I personally knew the folks being written about. There is much wisdom here.'

Long live odd titles, and long live the *Bookseller*'s Diagram Prize. If you ever spot a contender, send a note to bent@bookseller.co.uk. Fame and fortune awaits.

JOEL RICKETT
DEPUTY EDITOR, THE BOOKSELLER

# ACKNOWLEDGEMENTS

'I've made an odd discovery...'
*Bertrand Russell*

Thanks to Bruce Robertson of the Diagram Group, who started it all (and who continues to be a champion spotter). Thanks to Aurum Press, who had the wonderfully odd idea for this book of odd books. Thanks to all the staff of the *Bookseller* who have been involved in the prize over the last thirty years, particularly former editors Louis Baum and Nicholas Clee, current editor-in-chief Neill Denny, and the magazine's former information manager Colin Randall, whose diligent archiving made this book so simple to create.

But the biggest thanks are saved for the *Bookseller* readers who have suggested hundreds of odd titles and voted for their favourites. Those who spotted Diagram Prize winners were: Elfreda Powell, David Martin, Colin Eccleshare, Russell Ash, Sally Whitaker, Trevor Bounford, Mark Bryant, Desmond Elliott, Shad Helmstetter, Anne Tannahill, John Doyle, Stuart Booth, David Harris, Brian Shawcross, Simon Tuite, Nach Waxman, Nicholas Essen, Kate Santon, E.P. Kelly, M.J. Grant, Judith Seaman, Clare Gilliam, David Pearson, Mark Campbell, Neal Maillet, Jon Howells, David Evans, Graeme Henderson, and David Leonard.

# DESIGN FOR IMPACT
## 50 Years of Airline Safety Cards

Eric Ericson & Johan Pihl

*Princeton Architectural Press, 2003*

Illustrated coffee-table book about airline safety cards.

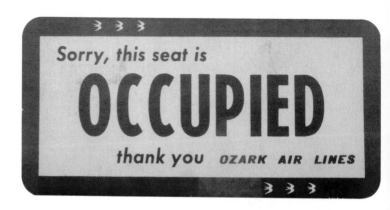

# OLD TRACTORS
## and the Men Who Love Them

Roger Welsch

*MBI Publishing Company, 1995*

Memoir of author's love affair with tractors.

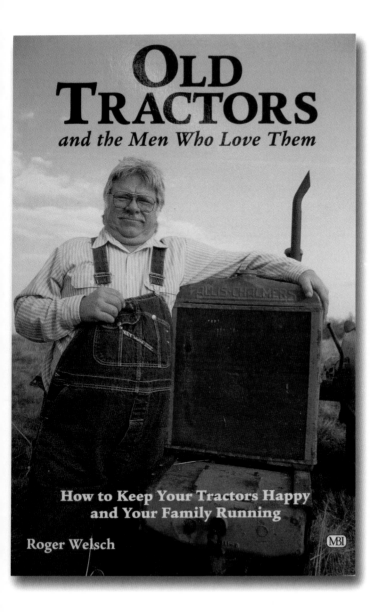

# OLD TRACTORS

## and the Men Who Love Them

**How to Keep Your Tractors Happy and Your Family Running**

Roger Welsch

# HOW TO AVOID HUGE SHIPS

## Captain John W. Trimmer

*self-published, 1982*

How to keep out of harm's way at sea.

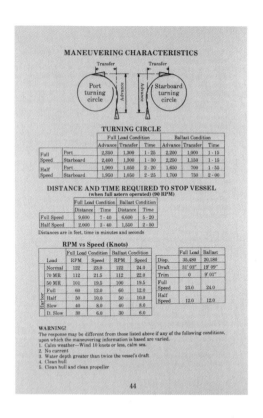

### MANEUVERING CHARACTERISTICS

#### TURNING CIRCLE

| | | Full Load Condition | | | Ballast Condition | | |
|---|---|---|---|---|---|---|---|
| | | Advance | Transfer | Time | Advance | Transfer | Time |
| Full Speed | Port | 2,350 | 1,300 | 1 - 25 | 2,200 | 1,000 | 1 - 15 |
| | Starboard | 2,400 | 1,300 | 1 - 30 | 2,250 | 1,150 | 1 - 15 |
| Half Speed | Port | 1,900 | 1,050 | 2 - 20 | 1,650 | 700 | 1 - 55 |
| | Starboard | 1,950 | 1,050 | 2 - 25 | 1,700 | 750 | 2 - 00 |

#### DISTANCE AND TIME REQUIRED TO STOP VESSEL
(when full astern operated) (90 RPM)

| | Full Load Condition | | Ballast Condition | |
|---|---|---|---|---|
| | Distance | Time | Distance | Time |
| Full Speed | 9,600 | 7 - 40 | 6,600 | 5 - 20 |
| Half Speed | 2,000 | 3 - 40 | 1,550 | 2 - 50 |

Distances are in feet, time in minutes and seconds

#### RPM vs Speed (Knots)

| | | Full Load Condition | | Ballast Condition | | | Full Load | Ballast |
|---|---|---|---|---|---|---|---|---|
| Load | | RPM | Speed | RPM | Speed | Disp. | 35,480 | 20,180 |
| | Normal | 122 | 23.0 | 122 | 24.0 | Draft | 31' 03" | 19' 09" |
| | 70 MR | 112 | 21.5 | 112 | 22.0 | Trim | 0 | 9' 01" |
| | 50 MR | 101 | 19.5 | 100 | 19.5 | Full Speed | 23.0 | 24.0 |
| Harbor | Full | 60 | 12.0 | 60 | 12.0 | | | |
| | Half | 50 | 10.0 | 50 | 10.0 | Half Speed | 12.0 | 12.0 |
| | Slow | 40 | 8.0 | 40 | 8.0 | | | |
| | D. Slow | 30 | 6.0 | 30 | 6.0 | | | |

**WARNING!**
The response may be different from those listed above if any of the following conditions, upon which the maneuvering information is based are varied.
1. Calm weather—Wind 10 knots or less, calm sea.
2. No current
3. Water depth greater than twice the vessel's draft
4. Clean hull
5. Clean hull and clean propeller

44

# HOW TO AVOID HUGE SHIPS
## OR
## I NEVER MET A SHIP I LIKED

by
## CAPTAIN JOHN W. TRIMMER

Master Mariner & Deep Sea Towing Master
Licensed Panama Canal Pilot
Active Washington State Pilot

NOT A COURSE IN THE
RULES OF THE ROAD

# NUCLEAR WAR: What's In It For You?

## Ground Zero War Foundation

*Methuen, 1982*

Everything you ever wanted to know about nuclear war.

Why do you feel scared with 10,000 nuclear weapons protecting you?

# NUCLEAR WAR

What's in it for you?

**GROUND ZERO**

## HOW GREEN WERE THE NAZIS?

Franz-Josef Brüggemeier, Mark Cioc
& Thomas Zeller (editors)

*Ohio University Press, 2005*

Environmentalism under the Third Reich.


## BEYOND LEAF RAKING

Peter L. Benson & Eugene C. Roehlkepartain

*Abingdon Press, 1993*

How to integrate
service-learning
into youth
ministry.

Edited by Franz-Josef Brüggemeier, Mark Cioc, and Thomas Zeller

# How Green Were the Nazis?

*Nature, Environment, and Nation*
*in the Third Reich*

# HIGHLIGHTS IN THE HISTORY OF CONCRETE

## Christopher C. Stanley

*Cement and Concrete Association, 1979*

Noteworthy developments in the history of the building material.

*Concrete work in ancient Egypt, c. 1950 BC.*

Cement and Concrete Association

*Highlights in*

# The History of
# Concrete

Christopher C. Stanley

# THE STRAY SHOPPING CARTS
# OF EASTERN NORTH AMERICA
## A Guide to Field Identification

Julian Montague

*Abrams Image, 2006*

How to identify abandoned shopping trolleys.

# THE
# STRAY
# SHOPPING
# CARTS OF EASTERN NORTH AMERICA

## A GUIDE TO FIELD IDENTIFICATION

JULIAN MONTAGUE

# WHAT TO SAY WHEN YOU TALK TO YOUR SELF

Shad Helmstetter

*Thorsons, 1986*

Self-help manual.

# WHAT TO SAY WHEN YOU TALK TO YOUR SELF

Powerful *new* techniques to programme your potential for success!

## Shad Helmstetter

# VERSAILLES
## The View from Sweden

### Elaine Evans Dee & Guy Walton

*Cooper-Hewitt Museum, 1988*

Exhibition catalogue.

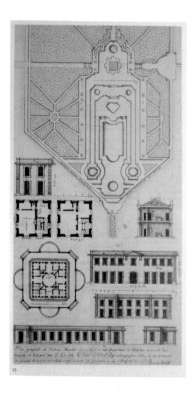

Versailles

The View from Sweden

# FABULOUS SMALL JEWS

Joseph Epstein

*Houghton Mifflin, 2003*

Collection of short stories.

# FABULOUS SMALL JEWS

*stories by* JOSEPH EPSTEIN

MARINER BOOKS

# GREEK RURAL POSTMEN AND THEIR CANCELLATION NUMBERS

Derek Willan (editor)

*Hellenic Philatelic Society of Great Britain, 1994*

An exhaustive record of the rural postal routes of Greece.

HELLENIC PHILATELIC SOCIETY OF GREAT BRITAIN


Publication Number 4


# GREEK RURAL POSTMEN AND THEIR CANCELLATION NUMBERS


Edited by

## DEREK   WILLAN

Price £20.

# ITALIAN WITHOUT WORDS

Don Cangelosi & Joseph Delli Carpini

*Meadowbrook Press, 1989*

How to communicate using Italian body language.

Common Expressions

**Help me, please!**
Aiutami, per favore!
(ay-OO-tah-mee payr fah-VOH-ray)

Now you can communicate in Italian
even if you don't know a single word.

# ITALIAN
# WITHOUT
# WORDS

Don Cangelosi and Joseph Delli Carpini

# THE BOOK OF MARMALADE
Its Antecedents, Its History and
Its Role in the World Today

C. Anne Wilson

*Pennsylvania Press, 1999*

All you could ever wish to know about marmalade.

C. ANNE WILSON

THE BOOK OF
MARMALADE

# THE ANGER OF AUBERGINES

Bulbul Sharma

*Spinefex Press, 1998*

Collection of short stories.


# THE JOY OF CHICKEN

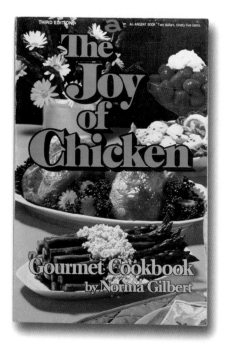

Norma Gilbert

*Argent Books, 1977*

Cookery book.

# the anger of aubergines

*bulbul sharma*

SPINIFEX

# ENTERTAINING WITH INSECTS
## The Original Guide to Insect Cookery

Ronald L. Taylor & Barbara J. Carter

*Salutek, 1992*

Cookery book.

## Dry Roasted Insects

Spread fresh, frozen, and cleaned insects on paper towels on a cookie sheet. Bake at 200° for 1-2 hours until desired state of dryness is reached. Check state of dryness by attempting to crush insect with a spoon.

## Basic Insect Flour

Dry roast insects (see preceding recipe) and blend in electric blender until a delicate flour is produced. The amount of flour resulting from a given quantity of dry roasted insects varies with the insect used. One cup of bees, for example, reduces to a smaller quantity of flour than does 1 cup of mealworms.

## Pastry

*For an 8-inch pie crust.*

1¼ cups flour
¼ cup bee flour (see preceding recipe)
½ teaspoon salt
½ cup shortening
4 tablespoons water

Mix together flours and salt. Cut in shortening with a pastry blender. Sprinkl with water, a tablespoon at a time. Mix with a fork until flour is moistened. Mold d into a ball. Place on a lightly floured b Flatten and roll out to about ⅛ inch t Keep pastry circular and roll it about larger than the inverted pie pan. Fol in half and transfer to the pie pan. U and ease pastry loosely into the pan. careful not to stretch. Trim pastry scissors ½ inch from edge of pan. F pastry under edges of pan. Flute th Hook points under pan rim. Fill a according to recipe being used.

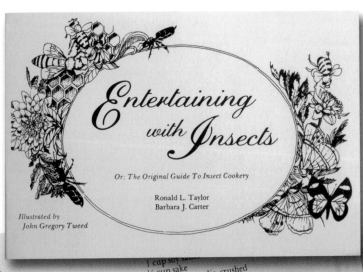

# Entertaining with Insects

*Or: The Original Guide To Insect Cookery*

Ronald L. Taylor
Barbara J. Carter

*Illustrated by*
*John Gregory Tweed*

1 cup soy sauce
¼ cup sake
1 large clove garlic, crushed
1 dried red pepper, crushed
2 tablespoons fresh ginger root, grated

Combine all ingredients.

To marinate insects, place them in the sauce for several hours, or if in a hurry, simmer for 20 minutes and cool.

## Garlic Butter Fried Insects

¼ cup butter
6 cloves garlic, crushed
1 cup cleaned insects*

Melt butter in fry pan. Reduce heat. Sauté garlic in butter for 5 minutes. Add insects. Continue sautéeing for 10-15 minutes, stirring occasionally.

*Mealworms are especially delicious prepared in this manner.

insects
t
e pepper
, diced
lemon juice

on butter
ns onion, finely chopped
parsley

all of the ingredients in a saucepan
g to a boil. Cover and simmer for
Cool and strain through cheesecloth,
ng firmly to express all the juices.
e. If less than 1 cup, add enough water
g to 1 cup. If more than 1 cup, boil

# THE SEXUAL POLITICS OF MEAT

Carol Adams

*Continuum, 1990*

Feminist-vegetarian critical theory.

# THE AESTHETICS OF
# THE JAPANESE LUNCHBOX

Kenji Ekuan

*MIT Press, 2000*

The lunchbox
as a key to
understanding
Japanese
civilization.

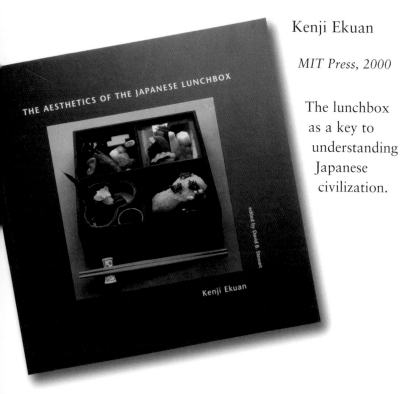

Tenth Anniversary Edition

# The Sexual Politics of Meat

*A Feminist-Vegetarian Critical Theory*

## Carol J. Adams

# BOMBPROOF YOUR HORSE

## Sgt Rick Pelicano

*J.A. Allen, 2004*

How to desensitize your horse to loud noises.

# Bombproof Your Horse

### Teach Your Horse to Be Confident, Obedient, and Safe No Matter What You Encounter

SGT. RICK PELICANO

with LAUREN TJADEN

# COYOTES I HAVE KNOWN

John Duncklee

*University of Arizona Press, 1996*

Memoir.

# 277 SECRETS YOUR SNAKE WANTS YOU TO KNOW

Paulette Cooper

*Ten Speed Press, 1999*

Manual for owners of snakes.

# RATS FOR THOSE WHO CARE

Dennis Kelsey-Wood

*TFH Publications, 1995*

Manual for owners of rats.

# 277 SECRETS

## Your SNAKE and Lizard

## WANTS YOU TO KNOW

Unusual and Useful Information
for Snake Owners & Snake Lovers

## PAULETTE COOPER

# THE CARE AND FEEDING OF STUFFED ANIMALS

## Glen Knape

*Harry N. Abrams, 1983*

Manual for owners of stuffed animals.

# The Care and Feeding of
# Stuffed Animals

### By Glen Knape

# KNITTING WITH DOG HAIR

## Kendall Crolius

*St Martin's Griffin, 1994*

Craft projects.

*Trevor loves the dog sweater made by his grandmother, Patricia Crolius.*

"For those who dread being in fashion's doghouse, there is hope—in the form of an all-natural fiber that can help you put on the dog." —*People* magazine

# Knitting

## WITH

# Dog
# Hair

Better a sweater
from a dog you
know and love
than from a sheep
you'll never meet

**Stop
VACUUMING
and START
KNITTING!**

**KENDALL CROLIUS** *and* **ANNE MONTGOMERY**

# KNITTING IN THE FAST LANE

Christina L. Holmes & Mary Colucci

*Krause Publications, 2001*

Craft projects.

# Knitting
## in the
## Fast Lane

◆◆◆
**More than
35 projects
for all skill
levels**

Christina L. Holmes
and Mary Colucci

# TEA BAG FOLDING

## Tiny Van Der Plas & Janet Wilson

*Search Press, 2001*

Craft projects.

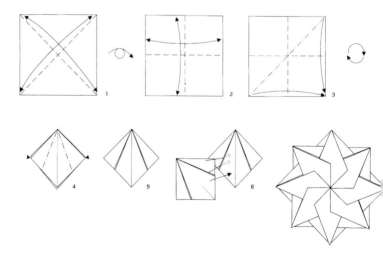

# TEA BAG
# FOLDING

*Tiny Van Der Plas & Janet Wilson*

SEARCH PRESS

# TOOTHPICK SCULPTURE & ICE-CREAM STICK ART

Bruce Bowman

*Sterling, 1976*

Craft projects.

*Built entirely of ice-cream sticks,*
*this giant Eiffel Tower model is shown*
*with its creator Keith Goodlander.*

# toothpick sculpture
# & ice-cream stick art

BY BRUCE BOWMAN

# DO-IT-YOURSELF BRAIN SURGERY
# & Other Home Skills

## Stewart Cowley

*Frederick Muller, 1981*

Fun projects to try at home.

**Crochet Your Own Suspension Bridge**

A full-scale replica of the Clifton Suspension bridge in crochet by Mrs Delia Etherington.

**You will need**
One 4ft crochet hook,
980,000 large buttons
1622 tons of 20-ply synthetic yarn
One 124ft crochet loom.

**Starting Work**

Neatness is most important when undertaking any large-scale work as it is extremely easy to get in a terrible muddle with the large quantities of yarn in use. Similarly, you should try to break down the project into predetermined sections to make certain that every aspect is completed satisfactorily. Every element in a suspension bridge has a vital function and the omission of even a seemingly minor part can affect the safety of the finished structure.

The safest and often easiest method, if you live close to the intended site for the completed bridge, is to work on the spot. Start by securely fixing two tightly plaited cables of yarn on large pylons at one end. Use rockets to fire the cables to the other side, cross, then fix these to the pylons there. Particular attention should be paid to the strength and fastenings of these cables as they will be the main supports for the final structure.

Once they are in place you must repeat the process with two further cables fixed at ground level. These will be the stringers for the actual road or rail tracks that will eventually be carried by the bridge. If the remaining fabric of the bridge is to be made on site you simply have to start at one end and work out towards the opposite side. If working elsewhere, remember to work in 980,000 buttonholes along the upper edges to provide a means of fixing the roadbed and suspension elements to the main guylines. It is well worth doing this anyway as it allows you to remove most of the structure easily for washing or cleaning at a later date.

Whereas working in place is quite straightforward, if you are working at home you will have to roll up the bridge as you complete each section. Quite a few people with a dislike of great heights prefer to do this, but remember that you will need a fair amount of free space to avoid any inconvenient tangling. Apart from this, the method of working remains the same in either case.

**Before You Start**

Decide the intended length of the project and calculate the relevant stress factors. Survey the final site to make doubly sure that your measurements are accurate. Although you can add extra lengths later if the bridge fails to reach the other side, it is quite likely that the additions will show and spoil the overall effect.

The correct technique for large-scale star stitch using ½" wool hawser and a golf club.

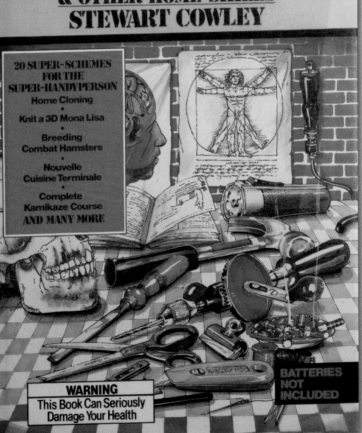

# DO~IT~YOURSELF
# BRAIN SURGERY
## & OTHER HOME SKILLS
# STEWART COWLEY

### 20 SUPER-SCHEMES FOR THE SUPER-HANDYPERSON

**Home Cloning**

•

**Knit a 3D Mona Lisa**

•

**Breeding Combat Hamsters**

•

**Nouvelle Cuisine Terminale**

•

**Complete Kamikaze Course**

**AND MANY MORE**

**WARNING**
This Book Can Seriously Damage Your Health

**BATTERIES NOT INCLUDED**

# WOOD CARVING WITH A CHAINSAW

Lyn Mangan

*Kangaroo Press, 1997*

Craft projects.

---

## WARNING

The instructions in this book are no substitute for proper training. Chainsaw carving should **not** be attempted by inexperienced chainsaw handlers. Seek professional advice **first**. Training courses are available—see footnote on p. 10.

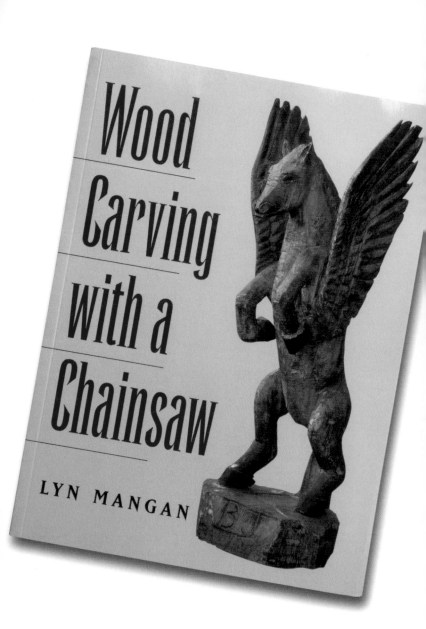

# Wood Carving with a Chainsaw

LYN MANGAN

# REUSING OLD GRAVES

## Douglas Davies & Alastair Shaw

*Shaw & Sons, 1994*

Research into public opinion on the subject.

| | |
|---|---|
| Soul passes on and Trust in God | 54 |
| Soul passes on and Reincarnation | 26 |
| Soul passes on and Resurrection | 21 |
| Resurrection and Trust in God | 11 |
| End of Life and Reincarnation | 8 |

*Table 8.10: Choice of Two Afterlife Beliefs.*

# REUSING
# OLD
# GRAVES

A Report on Popular British Attitudes

*by*

**Douglas Davies**

and

**Alastair Shaw**

 **Shaw & Sons**

# FANCY COFFINS TO MAKE YOURSELF

Dale Power

*Schiffer, 2001*

Craft projects.

# Fancy Coffins

## To Make Yourself

Dale Power

A Schiffer Book for Woodworkers

# BETTER NEVER TO HAVE BEEN
## The Harm of Coming Into Existence

David Benatar

*Oxford University Press, 2006*

Philosophical treatise.

OXFORD

DAVID BENATAR

BETTER NEVER TO HAVE BEEN
THE HARM OF COMING INTO EXISTENCE

# PEOPLE WHO DON'T KNOW THEY'RE DEAD
## How They Attach Themselves to Unsuspecting Bystanders and What to Do About It

Gary Leon Hill

*Weiser, 2005*

How to handle unwanted attention from the spirit world.

# People Who Don't Know They're Dead

G A R Y   L E O N   H I L L

# IS THERE SEX AFTER DEATH?

Jeanne & Alan Abel

*Bantam, 1982*

Film script for bawdy spoof.

# GOD MAKES SEX GREAT!

Dr Renier Holtzhausen & Professor Hennie Stander

*Metropolis Ink, 2001*

Self-help manual for Christians.

THE WILDEST
BAWDIEST, MOST
HILARIOUS SPOOF
OF THE SEXY 70s!

# Is There Sex After Death?

BY JEANNE AND ALAN ABEL

FULLY ILLUSTRATED
"LIKE THE MARX BROTHERS IN 'A NIGHT
AT MASTERS AND JOHNSON!'"
—METROMEDIA TELEVISION

# CELTIC SEX MAGIC
## For Couples, Groups and Solitary Practitioners

Jon G. Hughes

*Destiny Books, 2001*

How to practise Celtic sex rituals.

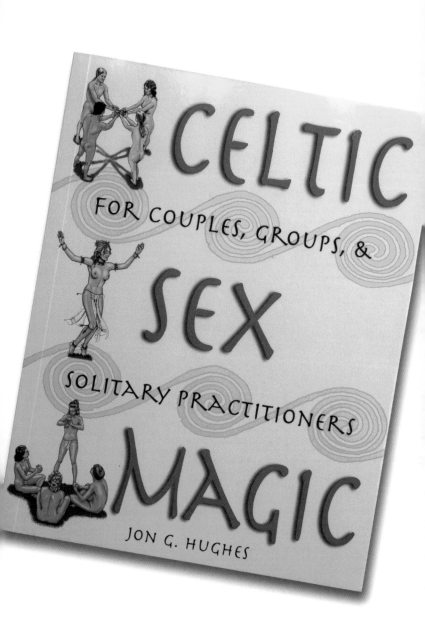

**CELTIC**

FOR COUPLES, GROUPS, &

**SEX**

SOLITARY PRACTITIONERS

**MAGIC**

JON G. HUGHES

## THE BIG BOOK OF
## LESBIAN HORSE STORIES

Alisa Surkis & Monica Nolan

*Kensington, 2002*

Collection of short stories.


## THE LESBIAN S/M SAFETY MANUAL

Pat Califa

*Lace Publications, 1988*

Tips for
practising
safe sex.

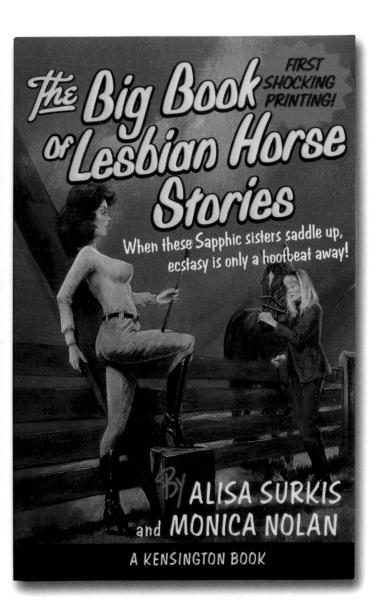

The Big Book of Lesbian Horse Stories

When these Sapphic sisters saddle up, ecstasy is only a hoofbeat away!

FIRST SHOCKING PRINTING!

By ALISA SURKIS and MONICA NOLAN

A KENSINGTON BOOK

# SIX-LEGGED SEX
## The Erotic Lives of Bugs

James K. Wangberg

*Fulcrum, 2001*

The sexual behaviour of insects.

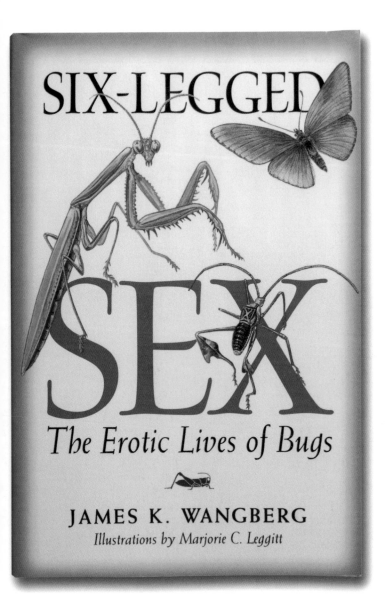

# SIX-LEGGED

# SEX

## The Erotic Lives of Bugs

### JAMES K. WANGBERG

*Illustrations by Marjorie C. Leggitt*

# CONFESSIONS OF A PAGAN NUN

Kate Horsley

*Shambhala, 2001*

Historical novel.

# AFTER THE ORGY
## Toward a Politics of Exhaustion

Dominic Pettman

*State University of New York, 2002*

Cultural theory.

# confessions
## of a
# pagan nun

*a novel*

kate horsley

# TATTOOED MOUNTAIN WOMEN AND SPOON BOXES OF DAGHESTAN

Robert Chenciner, Gabib Ismailov
& Magomedkhan Magomedkhanov

*Bennett & Bloom, 2006*

Illustrated record of a system of folk medicine.

# TATTOOED MOUNTAIN WOMEN AND SPOON BOXES OF DAGHESTAN

Magic medicine symbols in silk, stone, wood and flesh

Robert Chenciner, Gabib Ismailov & Magomedkhan Magomedkhanov

# READING TOES
## Your Feet as Reflections of Your Personality

Imre Somogyi

*C. W. Daniel Company, 1997*

Natural-healing manual.

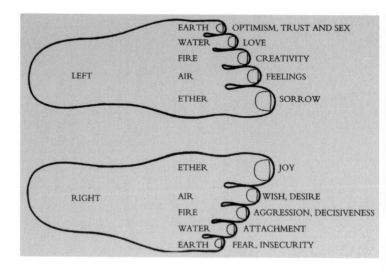

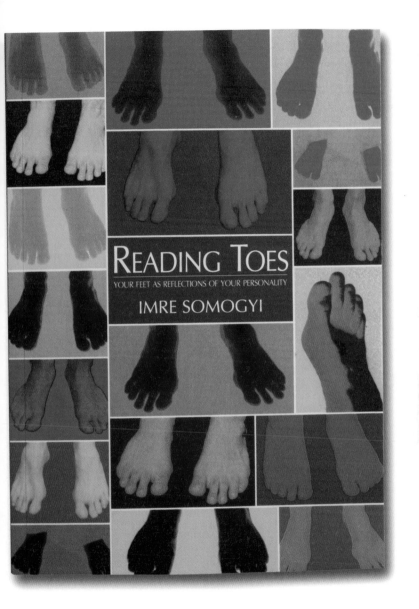

# READING TOES

YOUR FEET AS REFLECTIONS OF YOUR PERSONALITY

## IMRE SOMOGYI

# NATURAL BUST ENLARGEMENT WITH TOTAL MIND POWER
## How to Use the Other 90% of Your Mind to Increase the Size of Your Breasts

Donald L. Wilson MD

*Total Mind Power Institute, 1979*

Creative visualization techniques.

# DONALD L. WILSON, M.D.

# NATURAL BUST ENLARGEMENT WITH TOTAL MIND POWER

## HOW TO USE THE OTHER 90% OF YOUR MIND TO INCREASE THE SIZE OF YOUR BREASTS

## WHOSE BOTTOM?
A Lift-the-Flap Book

Moira Butterfield

*Ladybird, 2000*

Children's picture book.


## ARCHAEOLOGY IN
## THE AMERICAN BOTTOM

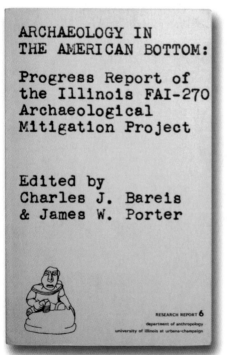

Charles J. Bareis
& James W. Porter
(editors)

*University of Illinois, 1981*

Archaeological project's
progress report.

Ladybird

1-3 years

Whose Bottom?

A lift-the-flap book

# LIVING WITH CRAZY BUTTOCKS

Kaz Cooke

*Penguin, 2001*

Novel.

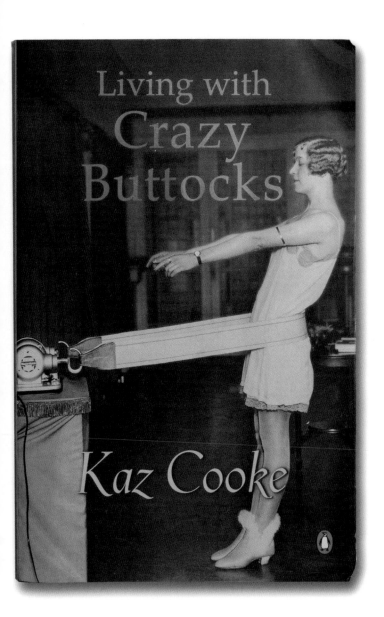

Living with
Crazy
Buttocks

Kaz Cooke

# HOW TO SHIT IN THE WOODS
## An Environmentally Sound Approach to a Lost Art

Kathleen Meyer

*Ten Speed Press, 1989*

Manual for fans of the great outdoors.

THE INTERNATIONAL BEST-SELLER WITH OVER 1 MILLION COPIES IN PRINT

2nd
Edition Revised

HOW
TO SHIT
IN THE
WOODS

An environmentally
sound approach
to a lost art

Kathleen Meyer

# OUTHOUSES OF ALASKA

Harry M. Walker

*Epicenter Press, 1996*

Illustrated coffee-table book.